DIY box creations

Fun and creative projects to make out of REALLY BIG BOXES!

by Courtney Sanchez

Quarto is the authority on a wide range of topics.
Quarto educates, entertains, and enriches the lives of our readers—
enthusiasts and lovers of hands-on living.
www.quartoknows.com

© 2016 Quarto Publishing Group USA Inc.
Published by Walter Foster Jr.,
an imprint of Quarto Publishing Group USA Inc.
All rights reserved. Walter Foster Jr. is trademarked.

Text and images © Courtney Sanchez
Photography by Clyde Sanchez
Page Layout by Elizabeth T. Gilbert

6 Orchard Road, Suite 100
Lake Forest, CA 92630
quartoknows.com
Visit our blogs at quartoknows.com

MIX
Paper from
responsible sources
FSC® C101537

Printed in China

1 3 5 7 9 10 8 6 4 2

table of contents

Introduction

Are you looking for great craft projects for the whole family? This book is filled with 12 fun and unique cardboard box projects you can create, with step-by-step pictures and easy-to-follow directions.

Have you just received a large package in the mail? Don't throw that box away! Cardboard boxes are a great building material. Create a stove, and play chef! Grab a box from the grocery store and turn it into a rocket ship so you can blast off and explore the universe. With a little imagination and an inventive spirit, the possibilities are endless.

 So roll those sleeves up! It's time to get crafty and create something money can't buy—memories.

Tools & Tips

While each cardboard project comes with its own supply list, here are a few basic tools you'll find yourself using regularly.

Painters tape is great for putting the pieces of your projects together. It's flexible and can be painted over easily.

Tips
- To prevent wrinkles, lightly apply tape and smooth from the center outward.
- When taping corners, cut a slit at the ends of the tape and fold it over to prevent sloppy edges and creases.
- Painters' tape is easily removable and won't cause damage; don't be afraid to remove the tape if you make a mistake.

Sample size paints from home-improvement stores are perfect for these projects. They are inexpensive, and come in any color you want.

Tip
After applying each coat of paint, use a blow dryer to ensure it's fully dry before adding the next coat to prevent the cardboard from warping.

Wood glue is the best glue for putting these projects together. It bonds well to the cardboard and helps make each structure more rigid.

Tips
- When adhering objects with glue, slightly rotate the objects back-and-forth against the cardboard for a better seal.
- Apply the glue in layers to prevent globs, and always keep a moist paper towel around to wipe off the excess.

Hot glue bonds quickly, making it great to use when slower-drying glues aren't strong enough.

Tips

• Always have a rubber mat (or another easily-cleanable material) nearby to set your hot glue gun on when not in use.
• Have someone hold the item being glued steady because hot glue dries quickly.

Spray Paint is perfect for small projects. It's quick to apply and dries fast!

Tips

• It's very important to spray in a ventilated area. Go outside, and use spare pieces of cardboard to prevent your work area from stray paint.
• Spray at least three coats onto the cardboard.

Crafting knifes allow you to cut straight, even lines through the cardboard. They work much better than a pair scissors! X-Acto is a popular brand.

Tips

• Always use a crafting knife with adult supervision.
• When cutting long strips of cardboard, it's best to place the pieces over a cutting mat to prevent unnecessary damage to your table, floor, or carpet.
• Use the tip of the knife to start the cut, but use the middle of the blade to continue.
• Keep a few spare blades around in case the tips break.
• Keep your hands away from the cutting area to keep them safe.

Getting Started

Remember, while these cardboard projects are fun for kids, an adult should always supervise and be the one to use the more difficult tools, such as a hacksaw, spray paint, and crafting knifes.

Many of these projects are slight variations of each other, so if you learn a few building techniques from one craft, you can definitely apply it to another. Go small, or get really, REALLY BIG!

airplane

The sky's the limit when using your imagination! Create a fun airplane in no time with just a few cardboard boxes.

You can travel to new places, fly across the Atlantic Ocean, or even become the next great stunt pilot! And when you're done playing, your airplane makes a perfect decoration for your room.

Supply List

- 2 cardboard boxes (16" x 16" x 15" and 18" x 18" x 24")
- Roll of painters' tape
- 2 wooden dowel rods (2½")
- Paint (your choice of colors)
- Pencil and eraser
- Fine-tip, black permanent marker
- Yardstick
- Crafting knife
- Large scissors
- Roll of 1" wide ribbon
- Hot glue
- 5 toilet paper rolls
- Large protractor
- Large number stickers
- Mini paper cup
- Paper party cup
- Brass round head fastener

Step 1 Let's start with the cockpit. Cut the top and bottom flaps off the 16" x 16" x 15" cardboard box with a crafting knife. *Make sure to keep all the scraps!*

Step 2 Create the plane's wings by cutting the 18" x 18" x 24" cardboard box in half with a crafting knife. Take one half, and cut it in half again to make two 18" x 42" rectangles. To round the wings, place the paper party cup on each corner, trace its outline, and cut with scissors. Next center the cockpit on top of each wing. Trace the inside of the cockpit onto the wings, then cut it out to create an empty square in the center of each wing.

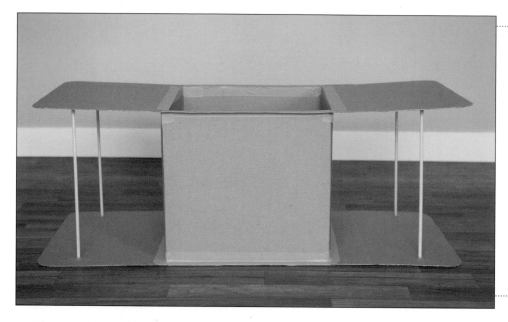

Step 3 Attach the wings to the cockpit using painters' tape. Be sure to tape both the inside and outside edges so the wings stay in place. Cut each dowel rod in half, creating four 15" tall rods. Hot glue the rods to each corner of the wings, 2" in from the front and 4" in from the side.

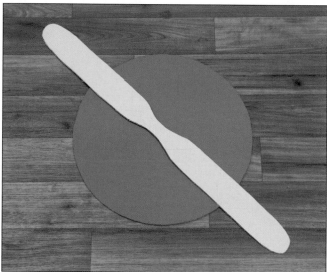

Step 4 To create the engine, use a protractor and scissors to cut out a 15" circle from a large piece of cardboard scrap. For the propeller, cut another piece of cardboard scrap to 2½" x 24". Draw a propeller shape, then use scissors to cut the propeller out. Apply two coats of paint to the front and back of the engine and propeller.

Step 5 Next paint the toilet paper rolls and hot glue them to the back of the engine. Push a round head fastener through the center of the propeller and engine, then fasten it in the back. Finally, paint your mini paper cup, and use hot glue to attach it to the propeller.

Step 6 To make the plane's tail, start by tapering the sides of two 15" x 24" cardboard scraps. On each side, draw a slanted line that starts 2" in from the edge and tapers off at the opposite end. Then cut along the line. The end result should be two pieces of cardboard with a 15" wide end and an 11" wide end. Attach the tail by taping the 11" ends to each other and taping the 15" ends to the back of the cockpit.

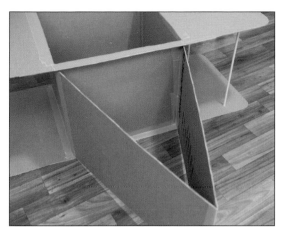

Step 7 Next draw and cut out the plane's fin. The front of the fin—the part that attaches to the plane's tail—should be 11" tall. Cut an 11" vertical slit near the front and a 4½" horizontal slit on the back, in the center. Then slide the fin over the end of the tail and tape it into place.

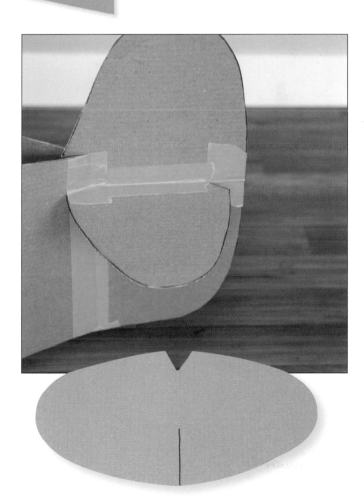

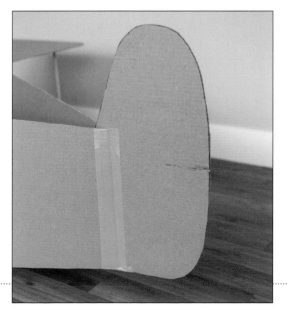

Step 8 Now draw and cut a 22" x 11" tailplane out of a piece of cardboard scrap. Cut a 4½" slit at the bottom of the tailplane, and slide it into the plane's fin, securing with tape.

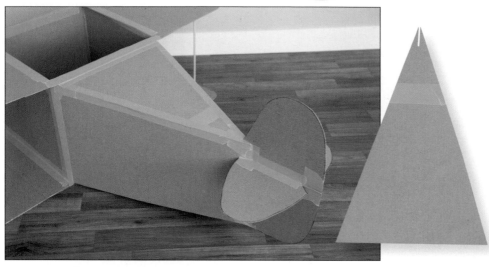

Step 9 To finish the plane's tail, place a large cardboard scrap on top of the opening, and trace the outline. (You may need to use two cardboard scraps and tape the pieces together.) Use scissors to cut out the triangular shape. Next cut a 1½" slit at the tip of the triangle and place it on top of the tail, sliding it into the fin. Tape into place, and close up the bottom of the tail with more painter's tape.

Step 10 Now the fun part—painting your plane! Cover the entire plane with paint. You may want to paint several coats to make sure the cardboard is completely covered. *Be sure to let each coat dry for 10 minutes!* Once dry, use your number stickers to decorate the sides of the tail.

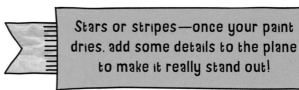

Stars or stripes—once your paint dries, add some details to the plane to make it really stand out!

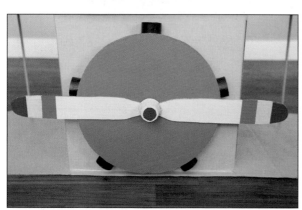

Step 11 Attach the engine and propeller to the front of the plane. Apply hot glue to the back of each toilet paper roll and stick them on the front of the cockpit. *Be careful—once you glue the rolls into place, they're not easy to remove!*

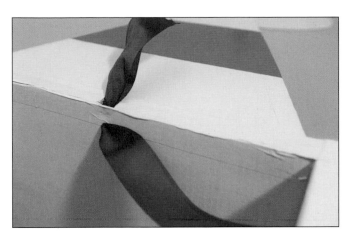

Step 12 Cut two 32" long strips of ribbon for the plane's shoulder straps. Make a notch in the center of the back of the cockpit, then cut a 1" vertical slit 1" below the notch. String the two strips of ribbon into the slit and up through the notch. Next cut two 1" notches in the front of the cockpit (about 3" in from each side) and a 1" vertical slit 1" below each notch. String each ribbon over each notch, through each slit, and into the cockpit. Knot each ribbon's end, and cut off any excess.

Step 13 To make a handle, cut a 12" long strip of ribbon. Then cut two 1" horizontal slits at the front of the cockpit, behind the engine. Knot the ribbon on one end and string it through one slit. String the other end of the ribbon through the remaining slit, tighten it, knot the end, and cut off any excess. Now get ready for take off!

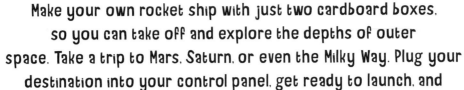

rocket ship

Make your own rocket ship with just two cardboard boxes, so you can take off and explore the depths of outer space. Take a trip to Mars, Saturn, or even the Milky Way. Plug your destination into your control panel, get ready to launch, and start your countdown. 5, 4, 3, 2, 1, Blast off!

Supply List

- 2 cardboard boxes (18" x 18" x 24")
- Roll of painters' tape
- Wooden dowel rod (½")
- Base paint (your choice of color)
- Secondary paint (your choice of color)
- White paint (optional)
- Chrome spray paint
- Sheet of green card stock
- Sheet of yellow card stock
- Pencil and eraser
- Fine-tip, black permanent marker
- Yardstick
- Crafting knife
- Large scissors
- Hot glue gun
- Assortment of milk jug and bottle caps
- Hacksaw
- Paper party cup

Step 1 Create your rocket ship's body by removing all the flaps from both cardboard boxes with a crafting knife. Stack both boxes on top of each other, and apply painters' tape where they meet (both inside and outside).

Step 2 To make the nose cone, take eight of the flaps from step 1, and tape them together on both sides in sets of two (creating a total of four squares). Use a marker to draw a straight line from each bottom corner to the center of the opposite edge, forming triangles. Next cut out your triangles with a crafting knife.

Step 3 Tape the bottom of each triangle to the top of your rocket ship's body (one triangle per side). Once all four triangles have been taped down, form a cone shape by pushing them together and taping the seams. Finally, apply painters' tape to the top of the nose cone to ensure each piece stays in place.

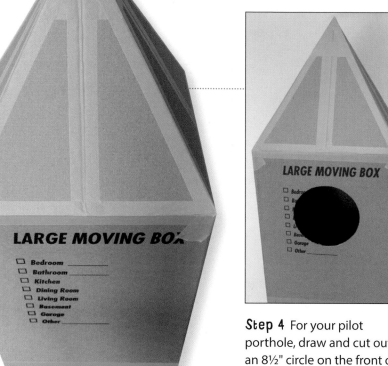

Step 4 For your pilot porthole, draw and cut out an 8½" circle on the front of the body (about 4" from the top) using a crafting knife.

Step 5 For the entrance, draw and cut out a large, full-length rectangle that's 3" from the top and 1½" from each edge on the side opposite the porthole. Round the top corners by tracing the outline of a paper party cup. Take care when cutting over the taped seams.

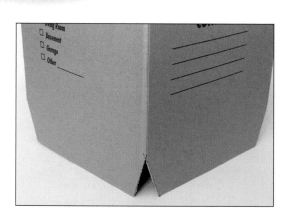

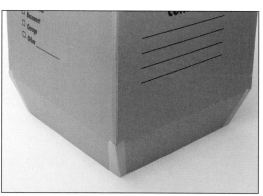

Step 6 To shape the rocket engine, use a marker to draw a triangle on each bottom corner of the ship's body (about 5" tall and 1½" from each edge). Cut out the triangles with a crafting knife and fold each side up and in, taping the inside and outside of the box with painters' tape.

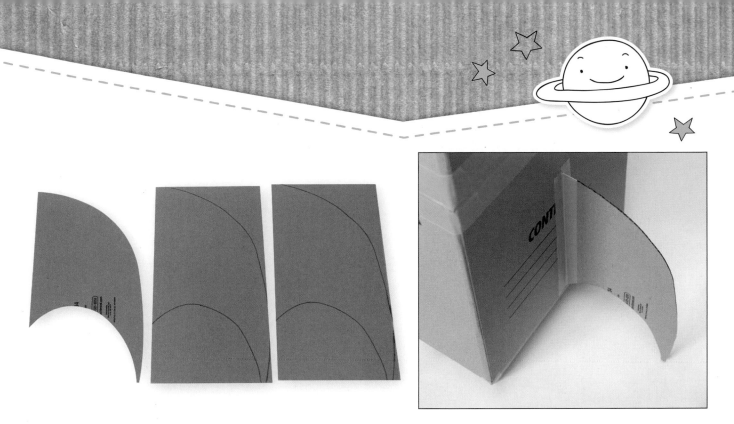

Step 7 Now it's time to create the rocket ship's fins! Take three of the remaining box flaps from step 1, and use a marker to draw a fin shape onto each one. Cut out the fins using a crafting knife. This rocket has curve-shaped fins, but any shape will work well! Attach your fins to the rocket ship by taping one to the bottom of each side. Be sure to tape both sides of each fin (this will make the fins easier to fold down when transporting your rocket ship).

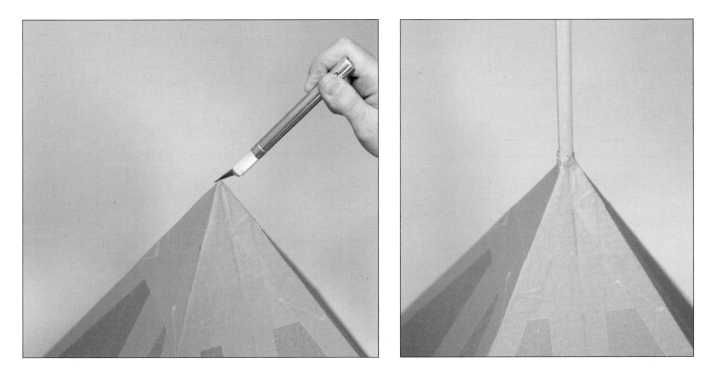

Step 8 Every good rocket ship needs radar! Take your wooden dowel rod, and cut it to 18" long using a hacksaw. Set it aside. Now cut four slits in the shape of an asterisk at the top of your nose cone using a crafting knife. Slide your dowel rod through the slits, and tape it in place (leaving about 4" hanging down inside the cone).

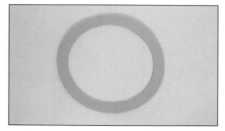
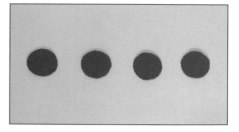

Step 9 Who's ready for some details? First create the passenger portholes by drawing and cutting out five 7" circles from a piece of spare cardboard. For the outer ring of the pilot's porthole (from step 4), draw and cut out a ring that has an outer diameter of 11" and inner diameter of 8½". Paint the ring and circles with your choice of accent color. For the rocket's fins, trace and cut out four 2" wide circles on spare cardboard. Then paint them the same color that you plan on painting your rocket ship's body. Set everything aside.

Step 10 Time to add some paint! Spray paint chrome details on the nose, radar pole, and bottom of your rocket. Paint three coats, letting each coat dry for 5 minutes. Let the final coat dry for at least 1 hour.

Step 11 Next paint two coats of your chosen base color on the rocket ship's body and two coats of your chosen accent color onto your rocket's fins. Then hot glue the portholes to the rocket ship. Finally, hot glue one of the small 2" circles to the top of the radar support pole and the remaining three circles to the tip of your rocket's fins. You can also add three coats of white paint to the interior of the ship if you like. *After applying each coat of paint, let it dry for at least 20 minutes.*

Step 12 To make buttons for the ship's control panel, cut about 20 squares (½" to 1" in size) from various sheets of colored card stock. Take the card stock squares, grab a few bottle caps, and set them aside.

Step 13 Now let's create the body of the control panel. Take one of the remaining box flaps, hold it up lengthwise, and cut it to about 5" wide. Take two more box flaps, and tape one to each edge of your 5" wide box flap. On one of the newly added flaps, cut off 1" (making the whole piece 8" wide). Leave the back of the 8" wide piece untaped.

Step 14 Next fold the control panel into the shape of a triangle (keeping the taped side facing in). Apply painters' tape along the outer seams, and spray three coats of chrome paint onto the largest side. Let each coat dry for at least 5 minutes, with the final coat drying for at least 1 hour.

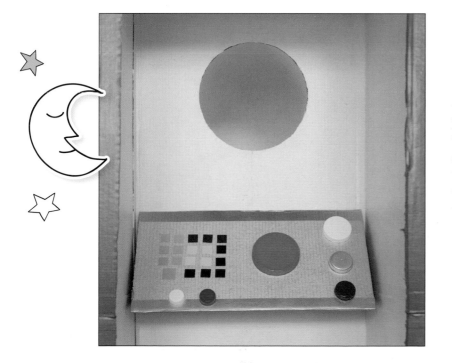

Step 15 Now hot glue your buttons and dials to the control panel. Finally, secure the control panel to the inside of the rocket ship using hot glue (at a height that's easy to reach).

boxcar

Cruise the open road (or your living room) with this cool cardboard car, based on the 1970 Chevelle SS Convertible. This car is perfect for any boy or girl—just customize it with your favorite colors, and you're ready to *zoom zoom!*

Supply List

- 4 cardboard boxes (24" x 18" x 18")
- 2 cardboard boxes (6" x 6" x 6")
- Cardboard box (18" x 18" x 16")
- Primary paint (your choice of color)
- Secondary paint (your choice of color)
- Accent paint(s) (your choice of color)
- Black craft paint
- Fine paint brush
- Paint roller or 3" wide paintbrush
- Silver, metallic spray paint
- Letter/number stickers (for emblems)
- Sheet of silver, reflective card stock
- Roll of painters' tape
- Fine-tip, black permanent marker
- 4 medium-sized paper party cups (your choice of color)
- Wood glue
- Large compass (or various sized circular objects)
- Crafting knife

Step 1 To begin, take a 24" x 18" x 18" box, tape all the flaps down using painters' tape, and then place on its side. Then draw a windshield on top of the box, leaving about 1" on each side. Make the windshield 10½" tall and 20" wide. (For a more realistic look, taper the windshield.) Cut out the windshield with a crafting knife, and fold down the remaining back flap, securing with painters' tape.

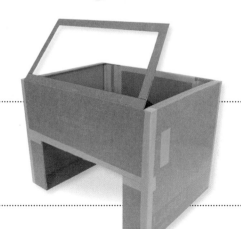

Step 2 Draw out a 16" x 9" rectangle on the lower front of the box with a marker, and cut it out with a crafting knife. Continue the opening by drawing and cutting a 16" x 18" square on the bottom of the box.

Step 3 For the front end, grab another 24" x 18" x 18" box, tape the bottom flaps down, and cut off the top flaps with a crafting knife. To create the tapered shape, draw two slanted lines on each side with a marker. The top lines should start at the cut end, 1" below the edge, and taper off at the taped end. The bottom lines should start 4" above the bottom edge and should also taper off at the taped end.

Step 4 Cut out the triangles, and tape the new edges together with painters' tape. Cover the opening using two of the 24" wide flaps from step 3. First tape the flaps together with painters' tape. Then measure the opening, and trim the taped flaps to match its height (around 13½"). Finally, cover the opening with the cardboard piece, and secure with painters' tape.

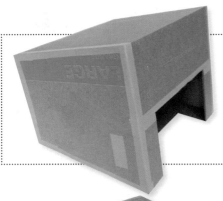

Step 5 With a marker, draw out a 16" x 9" rectangular opening on the bottom of the backside. Then continue the opening by drawing another rectangle of the same size on the adjoining, bottom edge. Cut along the lines with a crafting knife. This floorboard opening will be for your feet.

Step 6 For the back of the car, grab the third 24" x 18" x 18" box, tape the bottom flaps down, and remove the top flaps with a crafting knife (just like step 3). To create the tapered shape, draw two slanted lines on each side with a marker. The lines should start at the cut end, 2½" from the edges, and taper off at the taped end. Repeat step 4.

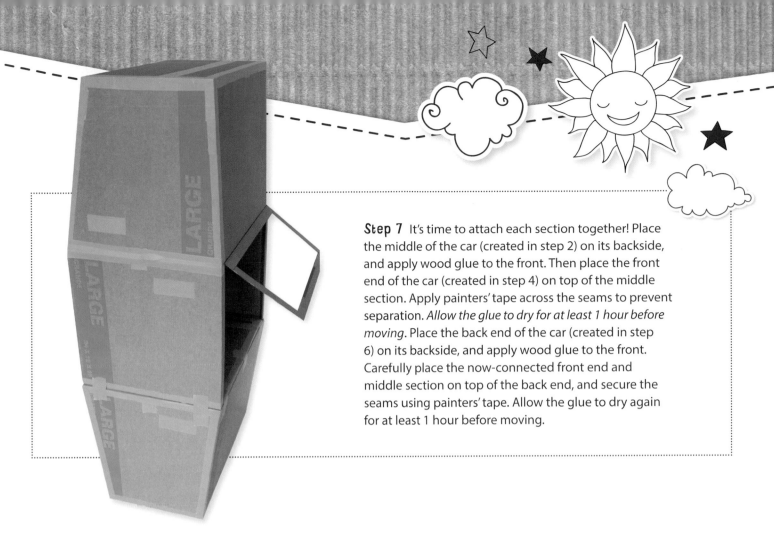

Step 7 It's time to attach each section together! Place the middle of the car (created in step 2) on its backside, and apply wood glue to the front. Then place the front end of the car (created in step 4) on top of the middle section. Apply painters' tape across the seams to prevent separation. *Allow the glue to dry for at least 1 hour before moving.* Place the back end of the car (created in step 6) on its backside, and apply wood glue to the front. Carefully place the now-connected front end and middle section on top of the back end, and secure the seams using painters' tape. Allow the glue to dry again for at least 1 hour before moving.

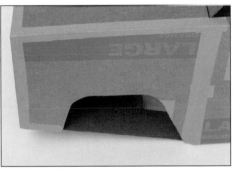

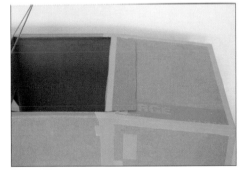

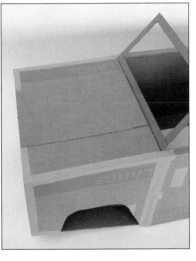

Step 8 Now on to the wheel wells. Place the car on its side. Starting from the corner touching the middle section, draw out an opening on the front and back end with a base width of 14" and top width of around 8½". Cut out the wheel wells using a crafting knife. Repeat on the other side of the car.

Step 9 To make the convertible top, grab a cardboard scrap that's 24" wide and around 4" to 5" tall. With a marker, draw out a trapezoid shape with a base width of around 22" and top width of 20". Cut out the shape using a crafting knife and attach it to the front of the back end (behind the seating area) using wood glue. *Allow the glue to dry for at least 30 minutes.*

Step 10 Now on to the hood scoop—grab your last 24" x 18" x 18" box, and cut out one side using a crafting knife. Cut the cardboard piece into a 12" x 18" rectangle. Finally, apply wood glue to the cardboard, and secure it to the hood of the car. *Allow the glue to dry for at least 30 minutes.*

Step 11 For the grill, tape together two 18" cardboard flaps using painters' tape (creating an 18" x 18" square). Trim the square into a 12" x 18" rectangle (with the tape running vertically) by cutting 3" from each edge with a crafting knife. Fold the center slightly, and place the rectangle against the front end of the car. The center should stick out roughly 1" from the car. Tape the edges to the front end using painters' tape, maintaining the triangular shape.

Step 12 Cut a 14" x 2" rectangle out of a cardboard scrap, and place it on top of the grill. Trace the triangular opening at the top of the grill onto the scrap piece with a marker, and then cut out the shape with a crafting knife. Tape it on top of the grill with painters' tape.

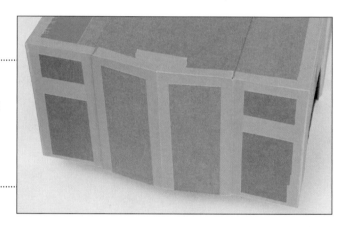

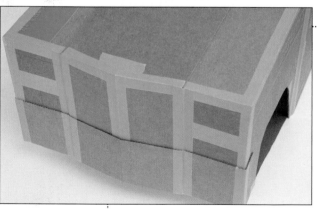

Step 13 For the front bumper, find two 24" wide cardboard flaps, and cut each to 24" x 6" using a crafting knife. Next cut one of the flaps into three pieces (6" x 6", 6" x 6", and 12" x 6"), and fold the longest piece in the center. From the remaining flap, cut two pieces measuring 2" x 6". Now attach each bumper piece to the bottom of the front end with wood glue. *Hold the pieces in place with painters' tape, and allow the glue to dry for at least 30 minutes.* Finally, cover your bumper's seams with painters' tape.

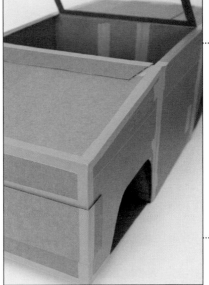

Step 14 For the back bumper, find two 16" x 9" rectangle scraps, and tape them together with painters' tape to create a 28" x 9" rectangle. Cut the rectangle to 28" x 6" using a crafting knife, and draw a 2" x 6" rectangle on each end. Score the lines with a crafting knife enough for the cardboard to fold, but not enough to cut all the way through! (This will allow the bumper to wrap around the sides of the car.) Apply wood glue to the backside of the cardboard, and stick it to the center of the back end. *Use painters' tape to keep in place, and allow the glue to dry for at least 30 minutes.* Finally, cover the seams of the bumper with painters' tape.

Step 15 Now it's time to add some chrome! Add three coats of silver, metallic spray paint to the following areas of the car: front end, both bumpers, front and back of windshield, and all wheel wells. *Let each coat dry for at least 15 minutes.*

Step 16 Now for the body paint! First tape off the headlights, grill, windshield, bumpers, and wheel wells to keep them silver. Next paint three coats of your chosen color onto the car's body. Once dry, carefully remove the tape. Now tape off the racing stripes and paint three coats of your chosen color. Once dry, remove the painters' tape. Finally, paint three coats of your chosen color for the convertible top and car interior. *Make sure to let each coat of paint dry for at least 15 minutes.*

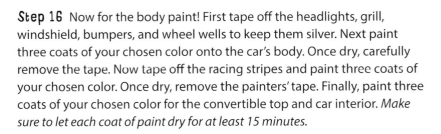

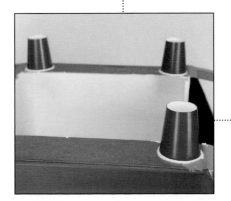

Step 17 To make it look like the wheels are supporting the car, take four medium-sized cups and glue them around the bottom opening with wood glue. For a better seal, twist the cups slightly after placing. *Allow the glue to dry for at least 1 hour.*

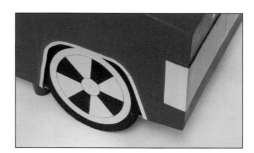

Once the details are drawn on each wheel, fill in the spots you plan to paint black with a marker so you don't accidentally paint the wrong area.

Step 18 For the wheels, grab the 18" x 18" x 16" box, cut off the flaps, and fold flat. Then trace four large circles (using a plate or large bowl) that are around 13" in diameter. Cut out the circles using a crafting knife, and set them aside. Add three coats of silver, metallic spray paint. *Let each coat dry for at least 15 minutes.*

Step 19 With a marker, draw a smaller circle on each wheel by tracing a small plate (or other round object). Next draw the rim details. Paint one coat of black paint where needed, and let dry for at least 15 minutes. Once dry, attach the wheels to the car by applying wood glue to the edges within each wheel well and firmly pressing each wheel in. Allow the glue to dry for at least 1 hour. *Wheels should be slightly above the bottom of the car's "feet" to prevent unnecessary bending.*

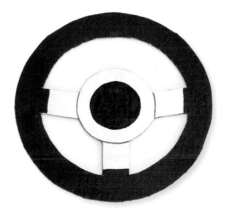

Step 20 For the steering wheel, cut a 10" x 10" square from a cardboard scrap. Draw a circle that's about 9" in diameter by tracing a small plate, and cut it out with a crafting knife. Draw and cut out the design for the steering wheel before painting it. If using chrome, paint three coats first. *Let each coat dry for at least 15 minutes.*

Step 21 For the steering column, paint a toilet paper roll with two coats of paint, letting each coat dry for at least 15 minutes. Draw a diagonal line around the roll about 1" from the top, and cut along the line with a crafting knife. Next glue the flat side of the roll to the back of the steering wheel. Finally, apply wood glue to the bottom of the steering wheel column, and attach it to the car's interior. Hold the column in place with painters' tape. *This part's tricky, but try to be patient.* Allow the glue to dry for at least 1 hour before removing the tape.

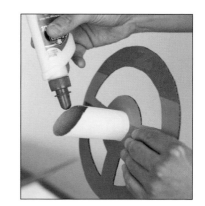

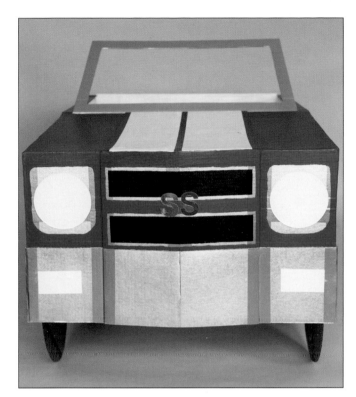

Step 22 Paint the grill, and add card-stock headlights. Since the 1970 Chevelle SS Convertible inspired this car, it has a few reflective SS emblems on the grill, as well as near the front wheel wells, the steering wheel, and the back bumper. Add chrome handles and key locks to the doors using silver card stock. Paint on front and rear blinkers and the edges of the car doors. Lastly, add the back bumper details (like taillights and a grill).

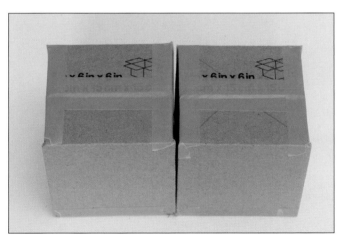

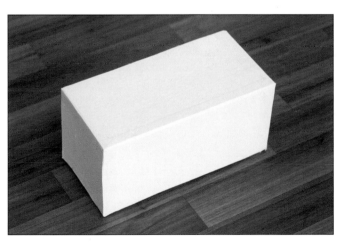

Step 23 This car is so close to being driven, you can almost taste the open road! Grab two 6" x 6" x 6" boxes, and tape each one closed. Tape the two boxes together, and paint the seat with three coats of interior paint. *Let each coat dry for at least 15 minutes*. Now you've got a removable seat for your super-sweet convertible. The only thing left to do is put the seat in, grab your keys, and peel out of here!

TRACKS

train table

Create an awesome table for your train tracks! Making this train table is quick and easy. The best part? It even has storage for all your tracks and accessories! Grab your conductor hat, a couple cardboard boxes, and let's get started!

Supply List

- 2 cardboard boxes (18" x 18" x 24")
- Roll of painters' tape
- 10 medium-sized party cups (your choice of color)
- Wood glue
- Crafting knife
- 2 ½" thick white ropes (12" in length)
- Yardstick
- Paint(s) (your choice of color)
- Scissors
- 2 sheets of green felt
- 2 sheets of brown felt
- 2 sheets of blue felt
- 3" wide paint brush (optional)
- Fine-tip, permanent marker (your choice of color)
- Medium or large sticker letters (optional)

Step 1 To create a strong tabletop, tape all the flaps on both boxes down with painters' tape. Do your best to prevent wrinkles and ensure the table looks smooth when painted.

Step 2 Lay both boxes on their sides, with the smoothest sides face up. Next tape the boxes together using painters' tape. Be sure the top of each box is even to ensure the train tracks will be level. For extra stability, wrap painters' tape around the entire structure to ensure the boxes stay firmly together.

27

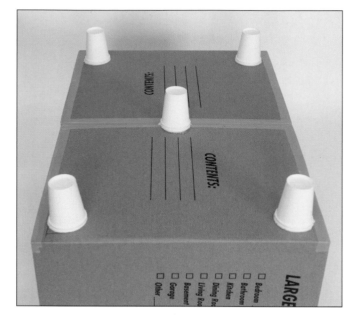

Step 3 To create the "feet," glue two party cups together with wood glue. (This ensures the feet are firm and solid.) Repeat this four more times to create five sets of "feet." Allow the glue to dry for at least 30 minutes. Using wood glue, attach a foot to each corner of the bottom of the table, about 1" from the edge, and one in the center. *Let the glue dry for at least 1 hour before continuing.*

Step 4 Now that the main structure of the train table is built, it's time to add the paint and details! First paint three coats (your choice of color) to the outer surface of the table, excluding the tabletop. *Allow each coat to dry for at least 15 minutes.*

Step 5 The next two steps are completely optional, but if you want to give your table the appearance of real wood, then lightly paint (also called "dry brushing") a slightly darker color around the table's base with a 3" wide paint brush. *Allow the paint to dry for at least 15 minutes.*

Step 6 To finish up the wood effect, draw faux wood slats around the table's base using a fine-point, permanent marker (your choice of color).

Step 7 Paint the tabletop with three coats (your choice of color). Let each coat dry for at least 15 minutes. *Be sure to tape off the edges with painters' tape for a clean line!*

Step 8 The train table is almost done! To create storage, cut out doors (16" x 12") on each end of the table using a crafting knife. Be sure to leave the bottom edges uncut, as these will act as "hinges."

Step 9 To add rope door handles, cut two "X" slits that are about 4" from the edge and 2" from the top of each door with a crafting knife. Feed each end of the rope into the slits and knot each end. Repeat for the other end.

Step 10 For the perfect touch, add labels like "TRAINS" and "TRACKS" using letter stickers. Just pick a font and color you like, and place them below the handles!

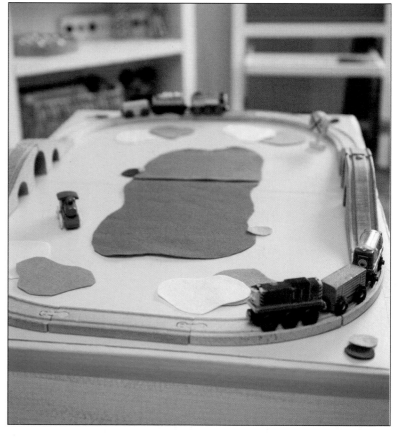

Step 11 Now this last step is also optional. If you'd like to have a few landmarks to place around the train table, pick a few blue, green, and brown felt pieces. Then cut water (blue), trees and bushes (green), and rocks (brown) from the felt with scissors.

hot-air balloon costume

Everyone should ride in a hot-air balloon at least once in their life (even if it's just in their imagination)! Fly up high over the sky with this super easy hot-air balloon costume made with a cardboard box and colorful balloons! Once you've finished, you'll be ready to go on one fantastical journey.

Supply List

- Cardboard box (18" x 18" x 16")
- Roll of painters' tape
- Wood glue
- 5 dowel rods (36" x ½")
- Ribbon (your choice of color/pattern)
- Black marker
- 4 clamps
- Crafting knife
- Small wood hacksaw
- Several sheets of paper (or tissue paper)
- 2 sand bags
- Helium balloon(s) (your choice of color)

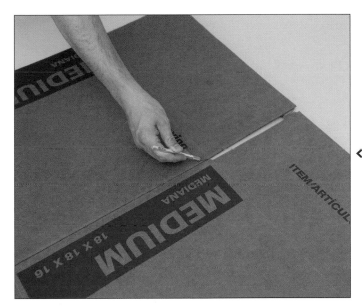

Step 1 To begin, deconstruct the box by cutting one of the seams with a crafting knife.

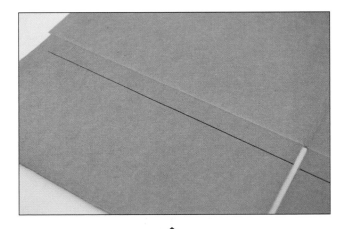

Step 2 Measure 1" from the bottom of each flap, and draw a line across using a black marker. Now trim off the flaps (8 in total) by cutting along the lines with a crafting knife.

 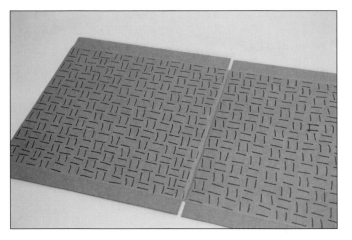

Step 3 With the box cut to the correct size, draw a basket weave pattern on the blank side of the box using a black marker. The pattern can be whatever you like, including this simple pattern mimicking the look of wicker weaving under and over the entire basket.

Step 4 Create the basket shape (with the weave pattern facing out), and apply tape to the inside corner of the box to hold the shape together. Be sure to apply the tape across the entire seam for a strong hold.

Step 5 Fold the top flaps over, and using wood glue, join them at the corners. Clamp each corner to hold in place. *Allow the glue to dry for at least 1 hour before removing the clamps.* Repeat this step for the bottom of the basket.

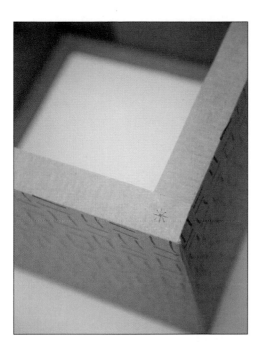

Step 6 Now let's add the uprights. Grab the dowel rods, and cut them to the following lengths: 26" (4x) and 18" (1x). Now cut four asterisk-shaped slits (the same width as the dowel rods) on each corner of the basket top. Then insert one 26" dowel rod 1" into each corner.

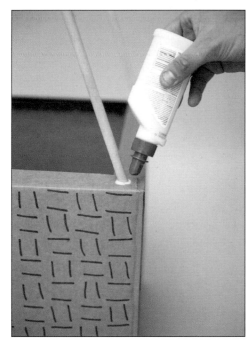

Step 7 Next apply a moderate amount of wood glue around the edges of each dowel rod. Be sure to wipe away any excess with a wet paper towel or cloth.

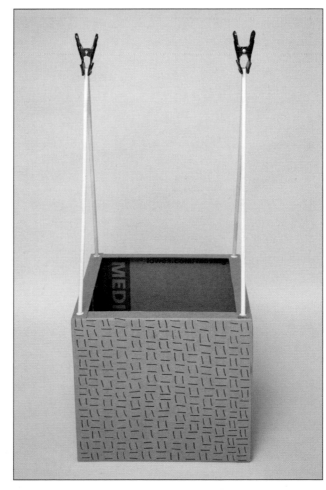

Step 8 Angle a pair of rods so the tops are touching. Repeat this step on the opposite side, creating two uprights in total. Now clamp the tops of each upright together. *Allow the glue to dry for at least 1 hour before continuing.*

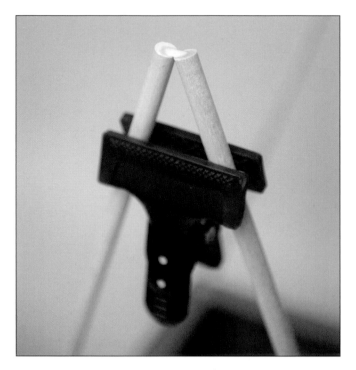

Step 9 Move the clamps about 2" below the top of each upright, and apply wood glue to the tops of the touching rods. Finally, place the remaining 18" dowel rod at the top of each upright to connect them, and add more wood glue to each side for a strong hold. *Allow the glue to dry for at least 1 to 2 hours before removing the clamps.*

Step 10 Time to add a few straps so you can wear this awesome costume! Cut two slits (the same width as your ribbon) on the front of the box, roughly 1" from the top and 4½" in from the sides, with a crafting knife. Repeat for the back of the box. Feed the ribbon straps about 6" through the front, and knot each end.

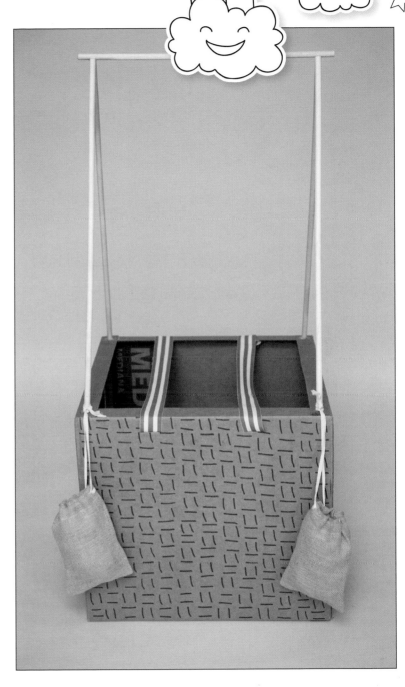

Step 11 Bring the ribbon over the top of the box, and feed it through the back of the basket. Then place the costume over yourself to size the straps, making sure the crossbar is roughly 4" to 10" above your head. Finally, knot each end, and admire your hard work.

Step 12 For the finishing touches, add a few sandbags (filled with balled up paper or tissue paper) along with some helium balloons. You can tie one BIG balloon or five to ten small ones—it's up to you!

indoor doghouse

Spoil your dog with a fun, trendy indoor doghouse that makes a charming addition to any room! This is a project the whole family can work on together to give their special friend their very own space. By using wrapping paper instead of paint to decorate the walls, the possibilities for patterns and designs are endless!

Supply List

- 3 cardboard boxes (24" x 18" x 18")
- Roll of painters' tape
- Crafting knife
- Roll of 30" x 12' wrapping paper (your choice of pattern)
- Yardstick
- Glue stick
- Hot glue gun
- Fine-tip, black permanent marker
- Cutting mat
- Scissors
- 20 sheets of 8½" x 11" card stock (your choice of colors)
- 16 sheets of 8½" x 11" white card stock

Step 1
Remove the bottom flaps from two of the cardboard boxes using a crafting knife.

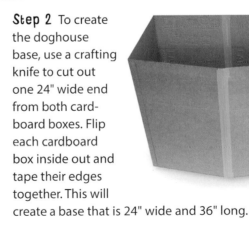

Step 2 To create the doghouse base, use a crafting knife to cut out one 24" wide end from both cardboard boxes. Flip each cardboard box inside out and tape their edges together. This will create a base that is 24" wide and 36" long.

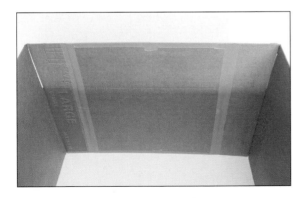

Step 3 Finally, to reinforce the sides of the doghouse, tape the two cardboard ends from step 2 to the center of each 36" long side using painters' tape. *Be sure to keep the flaps at the top—we'll be folding them in a later step.*

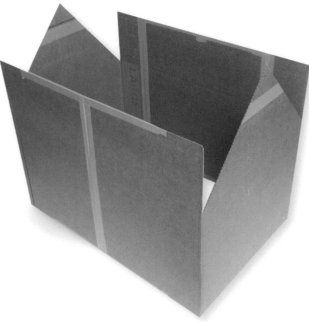

Step 4 For this next step, let's work on the roof of the doghouse. Cut a spare box flap into two 4½" x 24" rectangles. Tape each rectangle to the tops of the front and back of the doghouse using painters' tape. Draw two 18" lines that meet at the center to create a triangle shape on the front and back flap. Using a crafting knife, cut along the lines.

Step 5 To make sure the doghouse keeps its shape, we'll need to reinforce the inner corners of the big box. Grab a spare box flap, and with a crafting knife, cut out four rectangles that are about 2¼" x 24" in size. Next tape each rectangle to the inside of each corner. Finally, fold each side in, applying painters' tape where the edges meet the roof ends.

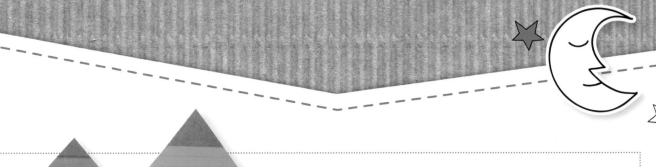

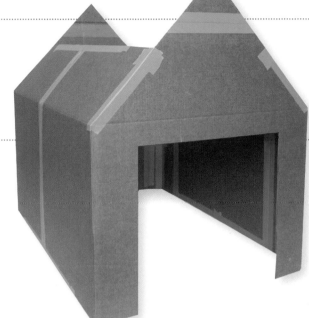

Step 6 Now we need a way for your pup to get inside! Create the entrance by drawing out a 16" x 16" square at the bottom-front of the doghouse. Next take a crafting knife, and cut along the lines to create an opening.

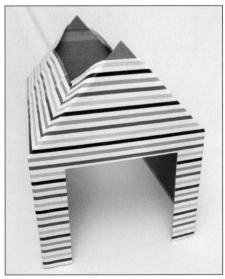

Step 7 Time to add some color! To apply a cool pattern to the outside of the doghouse, take the wrapping paper, and attach the end to the center of the back of the doghouse with a glue stick. Slowly unroll the paper around the entire doghouse, and add more glue every 6" to 12". Cut the excess with a pair of scissors.

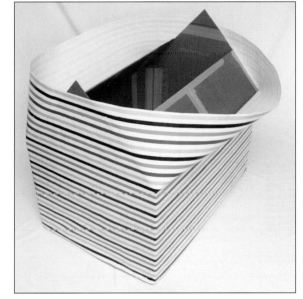

Step 8 Now lay the doghouse on its front side, and trim the wrapping paper from the opening using a crafting knife and a cutting mat. To tighten the paper across the roof, cut a slit at each corner with scissors and glue the paper to the roof.

Step 9 Cut triangles from the wrapping paper that are slightly larger than the bare spot left on each roof end. With a glue stick, attach each triangle and trim the excess.

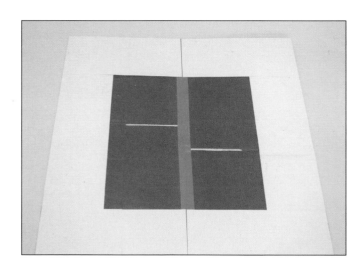

Step 10 Cut the remaining cardboard box into two even, large pieces using a crafting knife. Next cut each large piece to 20" x 40" in size. Tape the two 20" x 40" pieces together lengthwise with painters' tape (apply the tape to one side only). Now use a glue stick to attach white card stock around the edges of the roof's untaped side.

Step 11 Place your roof on the doghouse (there should a 2" overhang on the front and back ends), and secure using hot glue.

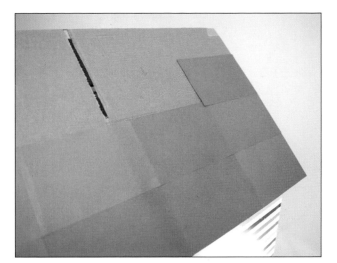

Step 12 Out of the 20 sheets of 8½" x 11" card stock (of your chosen colors), cut 15 of them in half to make thirty 5½" x 8½" roof shingles. Now attach each shingle with a glue stick, starting from the bottom and working your way over and up. Complete a total of three rows on each side of the roof, leaving the top row empty.

Step 13 To finish off the roof, take the remaining five sheets of card stock, fold them over the top of the roof, and secure with a glue stick.

Step 14 Finally, add some details! We opted for a dog bone sign above the entrance, but you can do whatever you'd like.

retro stove

You'll have tons of fun creating pretend meals with this cool cardboard box stove. You can customize this retro-style stove with just one large cardboard box, knobs that turn, and a baking rack! Want to create a whole play kitchen? Try making simple counters and cabinets to place on either side of the stove using additional cardboard boxes.

Supply List

- Cardboard box (18" x 18" x 24")
- Roll of painters' tape
- 2 wooden dowel rods (½")
- Base paint (your choice of color)
- Chrome spray paint
- Black acrylic paint
- Sheet of white card stock
- Sheet of silver card stock
- Sheet of black card stock
- Pencil and eraser
- Fine-tip, black permanent marker
- Yardstick
- Crafting knife
- Large scissors
- Hot glue
- Wood glue
- 7 milk jug caps
- CD
- 2 wooden skewers
- Hacksaw
- Paper party cup

Step 1 Create the base of your stove by cutting all four flaps off the bottom of the cardboard box with a crafting knife. Flip the box over, and tape the remaining flaps down to make the top of your stove.

Step 2 Grab a spare flap to form the stove's control panel. Using your party cup as a guide, round out the top corners of the flap. Tape the flap to the backside of the stove.

45

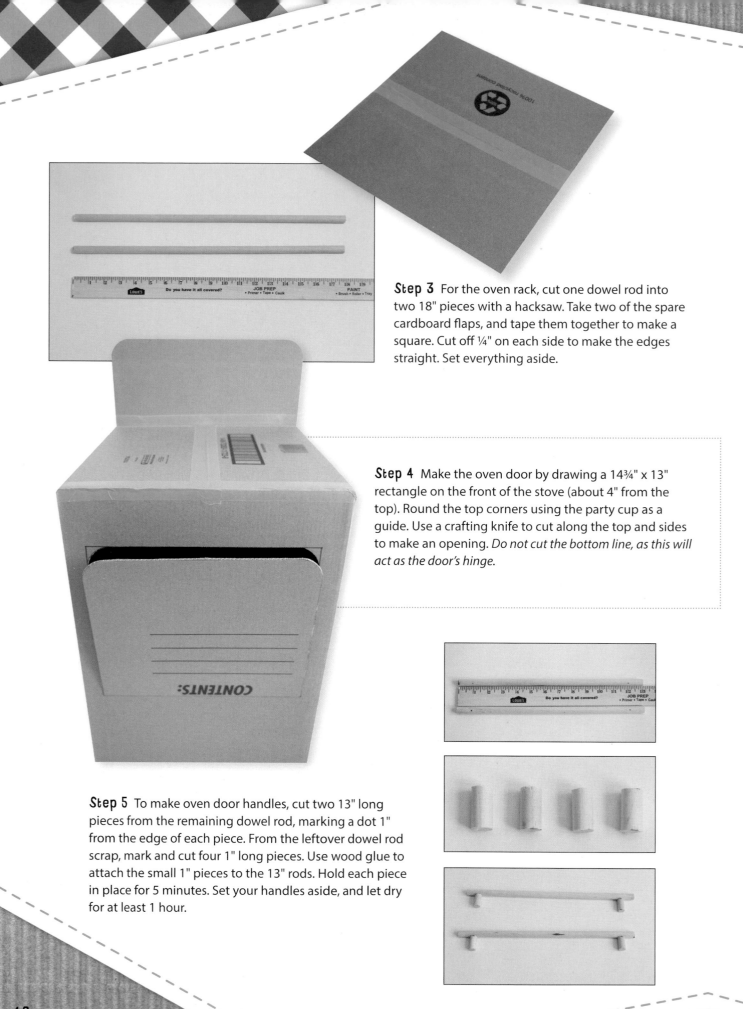

Step 3 For the oven rack, cut one dowel rod into two 18" pieces with a hacksaw. Take two of the spare cardboard flaps, and tape them together to make a square. Cut off ¼" on each side to make the edges straight. Set everything aside.

Step 4 Make the oven door by drawing a 14¾" x 13" rectangle on the front of the stove (about 4" from the top). Round the top corners using the party cup as a guide. Use a crafting knife to cut along the top and sides to make an opening. *Do not cut the bottom line, as this will act as the door's hinge.*

Step 5 To make oven door handles, cut two 13" long pieces from the remaining dowel rod, marking a dot 1" from the edge of each piece. From the leftover dowel rod scrap, mark and cut four 1" long pieces. Use wood glue to attach the small 1" pieces to the 13" rods. Hold each piece in place for 5 minutes. Set your handles aside, and let dry for at least 1 hour.

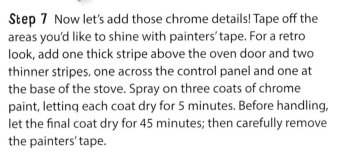

Step 6 Add some color! Cover the entire stove with three coats of paint (you can leave the back and inside unpainted, if you choose). *Let each coat dry for 15 minutes.*

Step 7 Now let's add those chrome details! Tape off the areas you'd like to shine with painters' tape. For a retro look, add one thick stripe above the oven door and two thinner stripes, one across the control panel and one at the base of the stove. Spray on three coats of chrome paint, letting each coat dry for 5 minutes. Before handling, let the final coat dry for 45 minutes; then carefully remove the painters' tape.

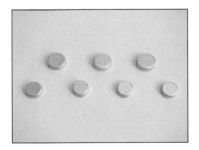

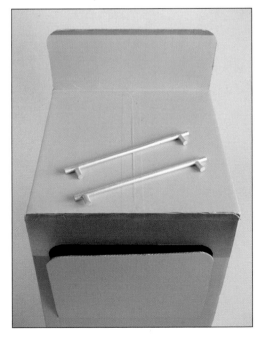

Step 8 Add three coats of chrome paint to all seven milk jug caps, as well as the oven rack and handles, following the same drying instructions from step 7.

Step 9 To create the burners, first cut out four 5½" circles from the silver card stock. Next use a CD to trace and cut four circles from the remaining cardboard box flap. Paint three coats of black acrylic paint onto the cardboard circles, letting each coat dry for 15 minutes. Hot glue each black cardboard circle to a silver circle, and then hot glue them to the stovetop. There should be about 2½" between each burner and the edges of the stovetop.

Step 10 It's time to attach the handles! Lay the stove on its backside and mark where you'd like to place the handles, one on the door and the other beneath the door. Take a crafting knife and cut four ½" slits in an asterisk shape on each marking (there should be a total of four). Add a thin layer of wood glue to the top of each asterisk and insert your handles. Being careful not to let the glue drip down the inside, rub any excess glue around each inserted handle (both the inside and outside). Add a few more drops of glue to each hole and smooth around each inserted handle. *Let dry for at least 1 hour.*

Step 11 Let's work on the knobs for our stove burners. Hot glue 2" pieces of wooden skewer to the back of each knob (you can also add wood glue to ensure the skewers don't pop off). Set them aside.

Step 12 Cut six small circles about 2" in diameter from black card stock. Hot glue the circles above the oven door. Using a crafting knife, cut a small asterisk shape in the center of each black circle. Gently pierce each asterisk with a wooden skewer to make a hole. Once done, simply insert your stove knobs, and you're almost ready!

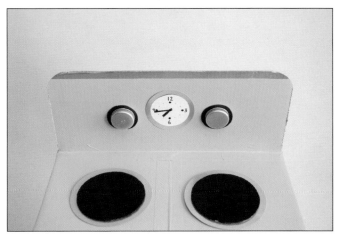

Step 13 To make your stove's clock, cut a 3" circle out of white card stock (use the inside of the painters' tape roll as a guide), and draw the clock face with a black marker. Cut a 3½" circle out of your remaining silver card stock, and hot glue the clock to the center. Lastly, hot glue the entire clock to the center of your stove's control panel.

Step 14 To add the last knobs, hot glue the two remaining black circles (from step 12) to each side of the clock. Mark the centers with a pencil, and cut small asterisk shapes on each using a crafting knife. Pierce each asterisk gently with a wooden skewer. To finish, simply insert your remaining knobs.

Step 15 To complete the stove, we need to add the oven rack. First lay the stove on its side, and then hot glue each remaining 18" dowel rod to the inner edges of the oven's center (one in the front and the other in the back). Then rub wood glue around the ends of each dowel rod. *Let dry for at least 1 hour.* Finally, stand your stove up, and rest the cardboard oven rack (chrome side up) on top of the wooden dowels.

dollhouse

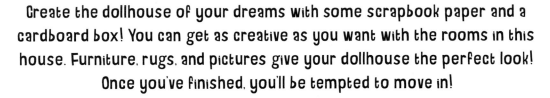

Create the dollhouse of your dreams with some scrapbook paper and a cardboard box! You can get as creative as you want with the rooms in this house. Furniture, rugs, and pictures give your dollhouse the perfect look! Once you've finished, you'll be tempted to move in!

Supply List

- Cardboard box (16" x 16" x 15")
- Roll of painters' tape
- 2 glue sticks
- Craft glue
- Hot glue gun
- Crafting knife
- Cutting mat
- Yardstick
- Standard size circle punch
- 4 push pins
- Fine-tip, black permanent marker
- 2 small, plastic beads
- White spray paint
- 4 sheets of 12" x 12" patterned scrapbook paper (two with the same pattern for interior walls)
- 20–23 sheets of 8½" x 11½ card stock for siding and inside molding (your choice of color)
- 4 sheets of 12" x 12" card stock for roof shingles (your choice of color)
- Sheet of 12" x 12" card stock for door and inside molding (your choice of color)
- Sheet of 12" x 12" card stock for outside molding
- 4 sheets of 8½" x 11" wood scrapbook paper for flooring

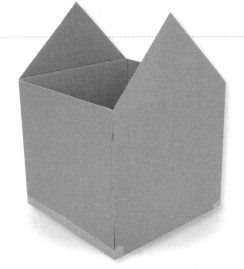

Step 1 To create the top of the dollhouse, cut off two opposing flaps from the top of the box. Next use a marker to draw triangles on the remaining two flaps. Cut along the line with a crafting knife. Now cut off two opposing flaps from the bottom of the box, and tape the remaining two flaps together to create the bottom floor.

Step 2 Draw the opening of the dollhouse, leaving a 1" edge on the sides and bottom of the box, and cut it out. Paint the interior by spraying at least three coats of white paint all the way to the top of each wall. *Let each coat dry for 10 minutes and the final coat for at least 1 hour before handling.*

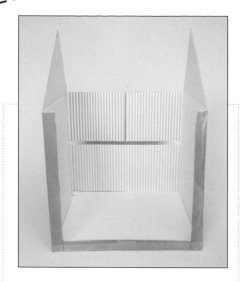

Step 3 To make the wallpaper, cut two sheets of patterned scrapbook paper to 8" x 8". Then cut the two remaining sheets to 8" x 12". Take the two 8" x 12" sheets and glue them to the bottom of the back interior wall (these sheets will overlap to cover the entire width of the cardboard). If needed, trim off any excess. Next glue the 8" x 8" sheets to the upper left and upper right portions of the same wall.

Step 4 Next cut two strips of white card stock to 1" x 11" and four more strips to ½" x 11". Glue the two 1" x 11" strips to the middle of the back interior wall (the horizontal, bare space in between the wallpaper). Glue the remaining ½" x 11" strips to the top and bottom of the back interior wall.

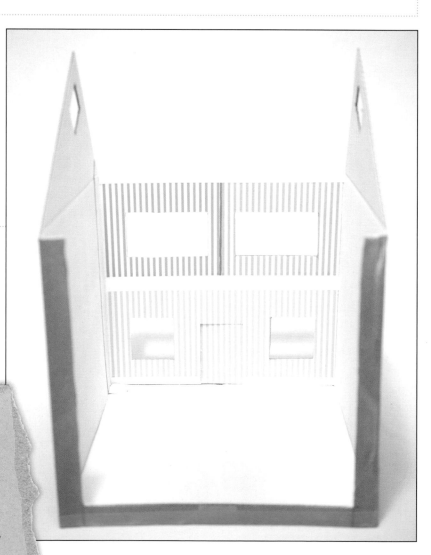

Step 5 Now it's time to create the door and windows! Draw and cut the front door of the dollhouse onto the back interior wall (it should measure 3" x 4½"). Make sure to leave the right side untouched so you can swing the door open. Next cut out the windows with a crafting knife.

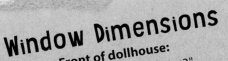

Window Dimensions
Front of dollhouse:
Two top windows = 5½" x 3"
Two bottom windows = 3" x 3"
Sides of dollhouse:
Two attic windows = 2" x 2" diamonds
Four side windows = 5½" x 3"

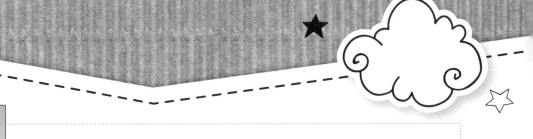

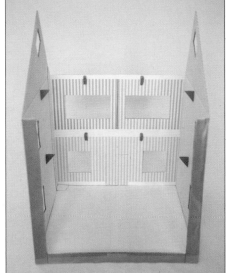

Step 6 For the floor supports, cut twenty-four 1" x 1" x 1½" triangles from a cardboard scrap (don't use a full flap, as you'll need them later). Take three triangles, and glue them together. Perform this step seven more times, making eight thick triangles in total. Hot glue the triangles to each floor (evenly spaced and four per floor).

Step 7 Next take the four sheets of floor scrapbook paper, and glue them to the bottom of the box with a glue stick. Start in one corner and work your way around in a clockwise pattern.

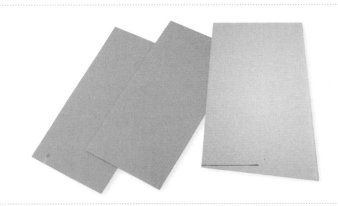

Step 8 Now let's create the upper floors. Grab two 16" x 8" cardboard flaps, and spray at least three coats of white paint on them. Let each coat dry for at least 10 minutes, then set them aside. For the wall partition, take another 16" x 8" cardboard flap, and draw a slanted line at the bottom to create a 1" tall triangle shape. Cut off the triangle. Next cut a 4" horizontal line directly above the shorter side of the edge you just cut.

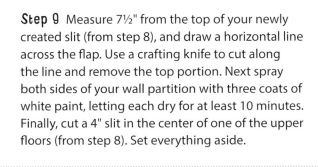

Step 9 Measure 7½" from the top of your newly created slit (from step 8), and draw a horizontal line across the flap. Use a crafting knife to cut along the line and remove the top portion. Next spray both sides of your wall partition with three coats of white paint, letting each dry for at least 10 minutes. Finally, cut a 4" slit in the center of one of the upper floors (from step 8). Set everything aside.

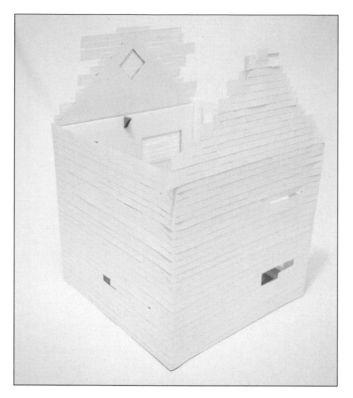

Step 10 To create the siding, cut 15 sheets of card stock into 1" wide strips. Starting from the bottom, attach the strips to the exterior of the dollhouse with a glue stick. Be sure to glue one row at a time. Repeat this step until the cardboard is completely covered. Now cut the excess card stock from the windows and the edges of the house with your crafting knife.

Step 11 To make the windowpanes, cut strips of white card stock that are ¼" wide and ½" longer than the windows. With craft glue, attach each strip to the window. Next create your inner and outer window moldings by cutting ½" wide strips of card stock with a crafting knife (from your chosen colors). The length of each strip should be 1" longer than the edges of the window. Attach each molding with a glue stick.

Step 12 Create your inner and outer door moldings by cutting ½" wide strips of card stock with a crafting knife. The molding for the top of the door should be 4" long, and the moldings for the sides of the door should be 5" long. Next attach the moldings with a glue stick. Use hot glue to attach two small beads to the interior and exterior of the door for knobs.

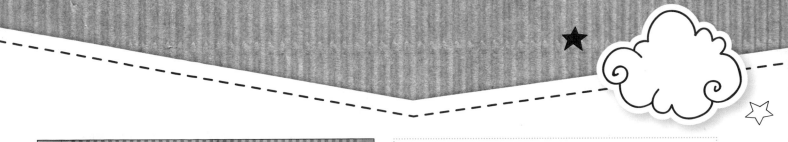

Step 13 Piece together the second floor and wall partition (from step 9). Then hot glue the two upper floors to each floor support. You can add hot glue to the top of the wall partition, as well as the side touching the back wall for additional support.

Step 14 To make the roof, locate the large cardboard scrap from step 2 and your last remaining box flap. Tape them together, placing painters' tape on both the front and back. Cut the cardboard to 17" x 12½" with your crafting knife, then attach two sheets of card stock to the backside of the roof with a glue stick. Finally, use your crafting knife to cut off any excess.

Step 15 For the roof shingles, use the circle punch to cut 1¼" circles (about 240) from four sheets of 12" x 12" card stock (of your chosen color). Next use craft glue to attach them to the top of your roof, starting from the bottom left and moving right, gluing a single row at a time. Repeat until the entire roof is covered. Once your shingles are dry and in place, flip your roof over, place it on a cutting mat, and use a crafting knife to cut a straight line down the left, top, and right edges. Be sure to keep the bottom edge for that pretty scalloped effect.

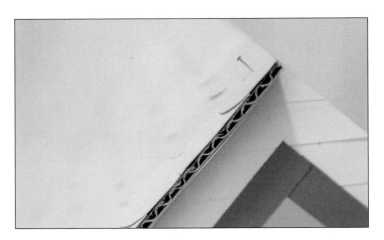

Step 16 Line up the top edge of the roof using two pushpins to ensure it's even. Hot glue (a line about 3" long) the top and bottom corners of the roof to the dollhouse, and hold firmly for a strong bond.

PUPPET
THEATER

Next Show
Starts
12:30 pm

puppet theater

It's showtime! Create your very own puppet theater in no time with just a couple cardboard boxes, and you'll have tons of fun putting on shows for all of your friends. Of course, it wouldn't be a puppet theater without the puppets. Create some of your own to star in the show—it's sure to be a hit!

Supply List

- 2 cardboard boxes (18" x 18" x 24")
- Roll of painters' tape
- Wooden dowel rod (½")
- Base paint (your choice of color)
- Fabric
- VELCRO strips
- Fine-tip, black permanent marker
- Yardstick
- Crafting knife
- Hacksaw
- Chalkboard sign
- Letter stickers
- Decorative glitter tape

Step 1 To create the body of the theater, take one cardboard box and remove the flaps with a crafting knife. Take the remaining box and cut off the bottom flaps only.

Step 2 On the second box, tape three of the four top flaps down, leaving the fourth up for the front of the theater. Stack the box on top of the first box, and apply painters' tape to where they meet (both inside and outside).

Step 3 Now it's time to make the theater's window. Measure out and cut a 15" x 17" square on the front of the theater (about 3" from the top) using a crafting knife.

Step 4 For the rounded top of the theater, trace and cut a large semicircle on the loose cardboard flap at the top.

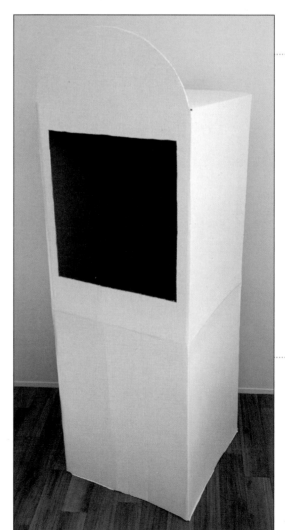

Step 5 Time to paint this theater! With your chosen color, paint three coats across the entire theater (leave the back unpainted for now). *Let each coat dry for 15 minutes.*

Step 6 Now cut out the theater's entrance. Take a marker and draw a horizontal line across the back, where the two boxes meet.

Step 7 Next cut along the line and the sides of the bottom box with a crafting knife. If you want to add some paint to the back and interior of your theater, cover them with two coats of your chosen paint color. *Be sure to let each coat dry for at least 15 minutes.*

Step 8 Pick out a fun pattern for your curtains! The fabric should measure 30" x 28½". Fold the fabric in half and cut down the middle to create two 15" wide curtains.

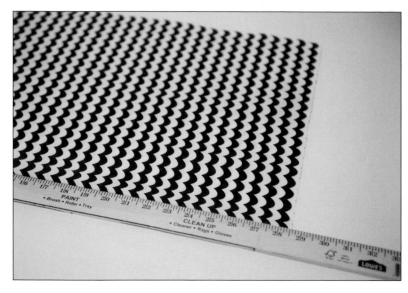

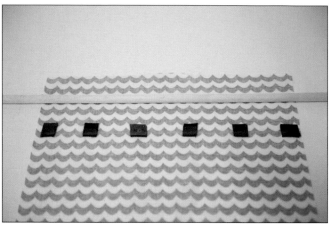

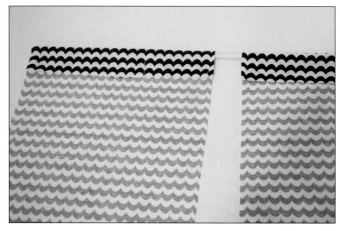

Step 9 Next cut the dowel rod to 21" long with a hacksaw. Lay the dowel rod on top of the backside of a curtain, and apply the VELCRO strips about 5" from the top of the fabric, leaving 1½" to 2" between each strip. Finally, fold the fabric over the rod and press against the VELCRO. Repeat the same process for the remaining curtain.

Step 10 Now cut four slits in the shape of an asterisk on each side of the top box, about 1" from the front edge, using your crafting knife (each slit should be between ¼" and ½" long).

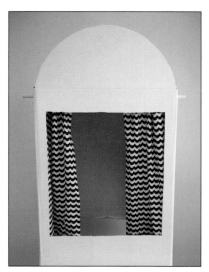

Step 11 Slide the dowel rod through the holes and hang your curtains. Once finished, you can paint the exposed dowel rod.

Step 12 Now the fun part, adding the details! For this theater, decorative glitter tape has been placed around the window and "Puppet Theater" lettering added with some stickers—but get creative and design your own letters if you're feeling up to it. Finally, grab a chalkboard and pin it to the front of the theater to display your show times. That's curtains, folks!

fort

Hide from Creepers in your very own Minecraft fort made from four cardboard boxes and some card stock. There's even a secret hideout and two cool hatches! When you aren't mining, this fort is the perfect place to read a book or play with toys.

Supply List

- 4 cardboard boxes (18" x 18" x 24")
- Roll of painters' tape
- Large, circular plate
- Fine-tip, black permanent marker
- Crafting knife
- Wood glue
- Glue stick
- 4 clamps
- Yardstick
- Cutting mat
- 50 sheets of various brown colored 8½" x 11" card stock
- 35 to 40 sheets of various green colored 8½" x 11" card stock
- Scissors
- 2' of green ribbon
- 1' of brown ribbon

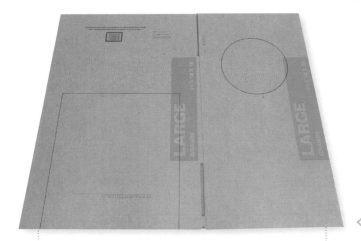

Step 1 To create the openings on Box A, first lay the box flat. Next use a marker to trace a large plate on the center of the narrower side (about 6" from the top). Then trace a large 20" x 18" rectangle on the bottom of the other, wider side.

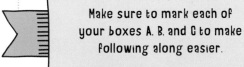

Make sure to mark each of your boxes A, B, and C to make following along easier.

Step 2 Flip Box A over, and trace a circle on the center of each side (about 6" from the top).

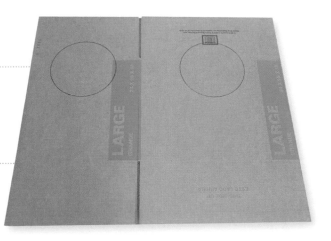

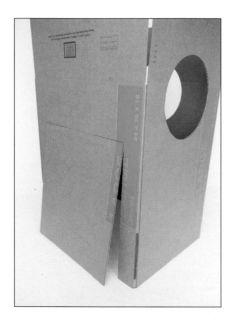

Step 3 Place your cutting mat down, and cut all the circles out with a crafting knife. Then cut both the vertical lines of the rectangle with a crafting knife, and fold up. Finally, pop Box A open, stand it up, and set it aside.

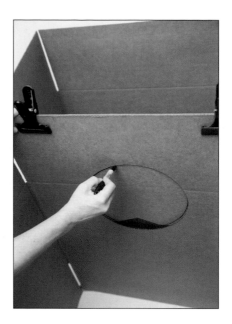

Step 4 Now take Box B, open it up, and use two clamps to attach it to the right side (the side opposite the rectangular opening) of Box A. Then trace the circle from Box A onto Box B. Remove the clamps, flatten Box B, and lay it on its side with the circle facing down.

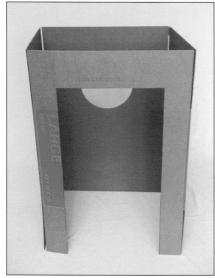

Step 5 Draw a large 30" x 16" rectangle at the bottom of the side opposite the circular opening. Now cut out the circle and rectangle, pop Box B open, and set it aside.

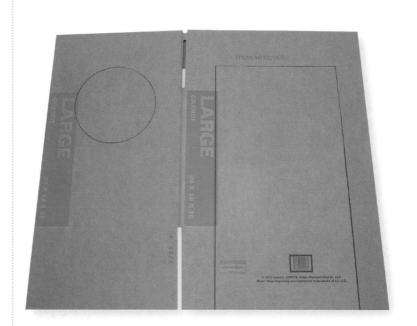

Step 6 To make the final "room" of the fort, place Box C down and draw a large circle on the narrower side (6" from the top). Then draw a 30" x 16" rectangle on the bottom of the other, wider side.

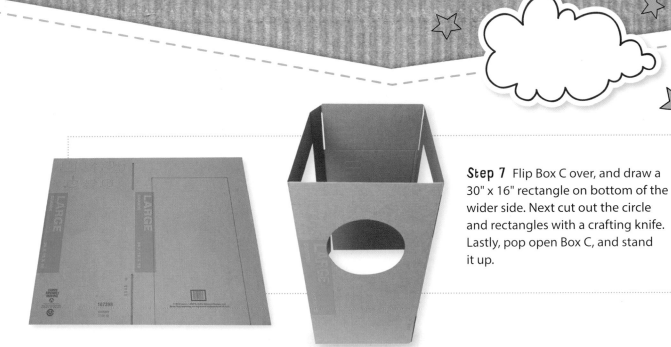

Step 7 Flip Box C over, and draw a 30" x 16" rectangle on bottom of the wider side. Next cut out the circle and rectangles with a crafting knife. Lastly, pop open Box C, and stand it up.

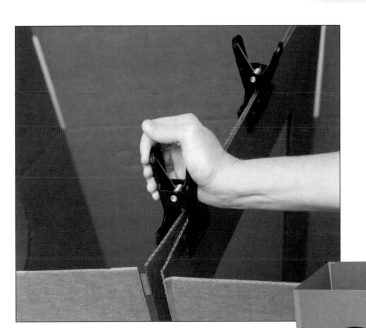

Step 8 To create the fort structure, take all three boxes and line them up in this order: A, B, and C. Now apply wood glue to the right side of Box A, and push Box B's left side up against it. Clamp the sides together. Repeat this step for Box B and C.

Step 9 Let the glue dry for at least 2 hours (overnight would be best). Once dry, remove the clamps, cover the seams with painters' tape, and admire your handiwork!

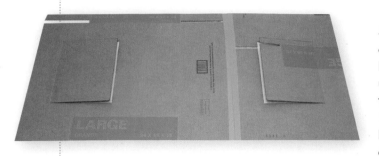

Step 10 Now on to the roof! Take the remaining box, and cut it in half with a crafting knife. (This will give you two large pieces that have both a narrow and wide side.) Now use painters' tape to join the two halves together. Then cut the roof to 57" x 26" with a crafting knife. Finally, draw a 12" x 10" hatch at each end of the roof, and cut along the lines with a crafting knife. Then fold up the uncut edges to create "hinges" for each hatch.

Step 11 Apply wood glue to the top of the fort, and place the roof on top. Set a few books or magazines (anything flat that adds some weight) on top of the roof where it touches the fort. *Let the glue dry for at least two hours.*

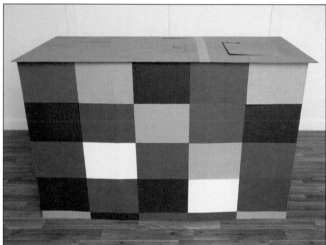

Step 12 Time to add our Minecraft pixel blocks! First grab a sheet of brown card stock, and attach it to the front of the fort (starting in the upper left-hand corner) with a glue stick. Continue gluing random brown-colored card stock, going left to right and continuing downward until the front side of the fort is completely covered. Repeat for the sides of the fort.

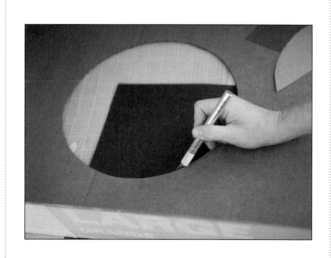

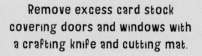
Remove excess card stock covering doors and windows with a crafting knife and cutting mat.

Step 13 Attach random sheets of green card stock to the top of the roof with a glue stick. When applying card stock to the hatches, be sure to cut the edges with a crafting knife.

Step 14 Now we can add our "vines" using more green card stock. First cut the green card stock into different sizes, making some short and others long, and fold the paper about 1" from the edge of the roof. Then use a glue stick to attach the folded card stock so it hangs down the edges of the front and sides of the fort.

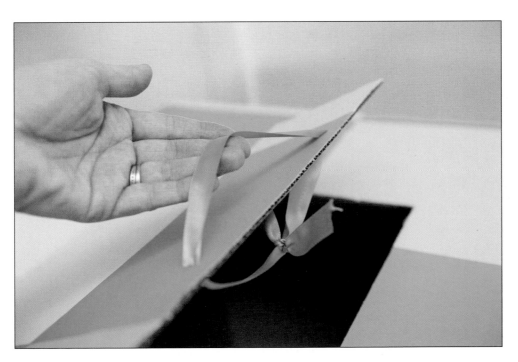

Step 15 To add handles to the hatches, take green ribbon and cut it into two 12" pieces. Now cut two slits on the underside of one of the hatches (about 5" apart). Then slide the ribbon through the slits, and knot the ends together. Repeat this step for all remaining hatches, using brown ribbon instead of green for the sides.

lemonade stand

"When life gives you lemons, make lemonade." But before you do, make a lemonade stand! Create the perfect place to share some yummy lemonade, adding little details to make your stand unique!

This lemonade stand is easily portable. You can set it up in your front yard, at the park, or even at a friend's house! Now that's a pretty fancy lemonade stand!

Supply List

- 3 cardboard boxes (18" x 18" x 24")
- Roll of painters' tape
- Crafting knife
- Pencil
- White paint
- Secondary paint(s) (your choice of color)
- Accent paint(s) (your choice of color)
- Large letter cutouts (your choice of color)
- 2 PVC pipes (1" x 60")
- 4 clamps
- Medium-sized paint brush
- Fine-tip paint brush
- Gorilla Glue
- Wood glue

Step 1 Take two cardboard boxes, and tape the flaps down with painters' tape. Be sure to cover every seam to ensure the boxes are nice and strong!

Your secondary paint colors will be used for the stripes and tabletop of your lemonade stand, while the accent paint will be used for the sign.

Step 2 With the smoothest sides face up, tape the two boxes together with painters' tape to make a single structure, applying the tape across the tops, bottoms, and around the center seam to solidify the structure.

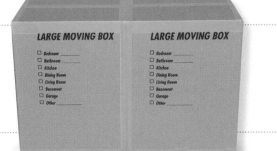

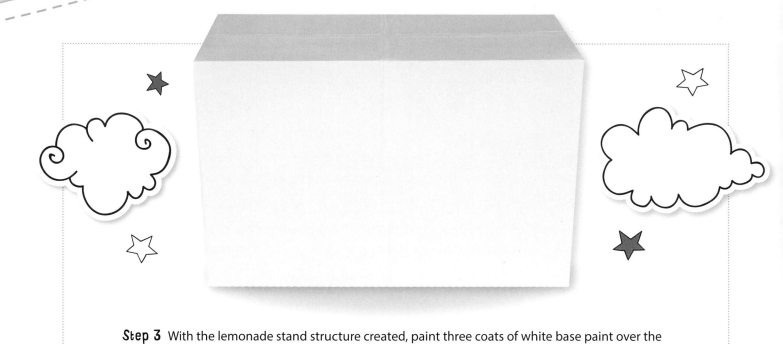

Step 3 With the lemonade stand structure created, paint three coats of white base paint over the entire surface (you can leave the bottom unpainted). *Let each coat dry for at least 15 minutes.*

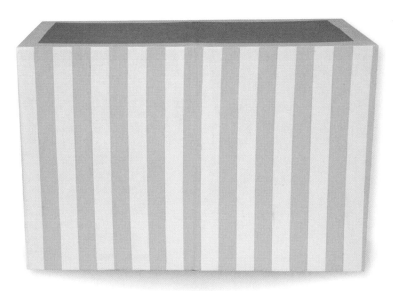

Step 4 To paint the decorative stripes, first add strips of painters' tape down the sides and around the tabletop. Next add three coats of your chosen secondary color across the stripes, letting each coat dry for at least 15 minutes. After painting the stripes, paint three coats of your other secondary color to the tabletop. *Let each coat dry for at least 15 minutes.* Once dry, carefully remove the tape to show off the stripes!

Step 5 Now it's time to add the poles for the sign. Place one PVC pipe over each front corner of the lemonade stand (about 1" from both edges). Then lightly trace a circle around the pipes with a pencil.

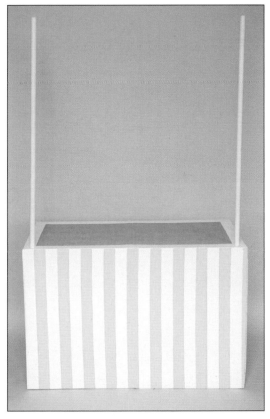

Step 6 Cut a large asterisk shape within each circle using a crafting knife, and slide each pipe into the asterisk until it reaches the bottom of the stand. (This will keep the poles and sign firmly in place.) You can also add a few dabs of Gorilla Glue around the base of each pole for extra support if you like.

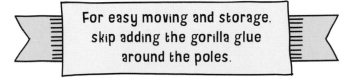

For easy moving and storage, skip adding the gorilla glue around the poles.

Step 7 For the sign, take the remaining cardboard box, lay it flat, and cut a rectangle that's about 36" x 12" using a crafting knife. Next paint three coats of white paint on the front and back of the sign. *Let each coat dry for at least 15 minutes.*

Step 8 To keep the sign rigid, add a 16" x 3" strip of cardboard to the back using wood glue. Let the glue dry for at least 30 minutes, then paint three coats of white paint over the strip. *Let each coat dry for at least 15 minutes.*

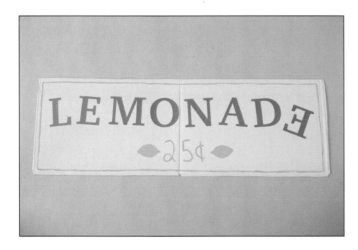

Step 9 Now add the sign's details. Add "LEMONADE" with paper letters or paint "25¢" with a couple lemons beside it. This part is totally unique to you, so have fun and make it cute!

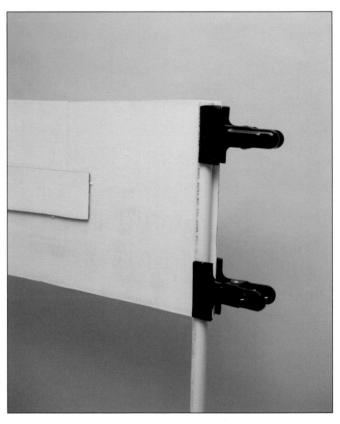

Step 10 With Gorilla Glue, attach the sign to the top of each pole. Keep it in place with a few clamps. *Let the glue dry for at least 2 hours.* Then remove the clamps, and get ready to sell some lemonade!

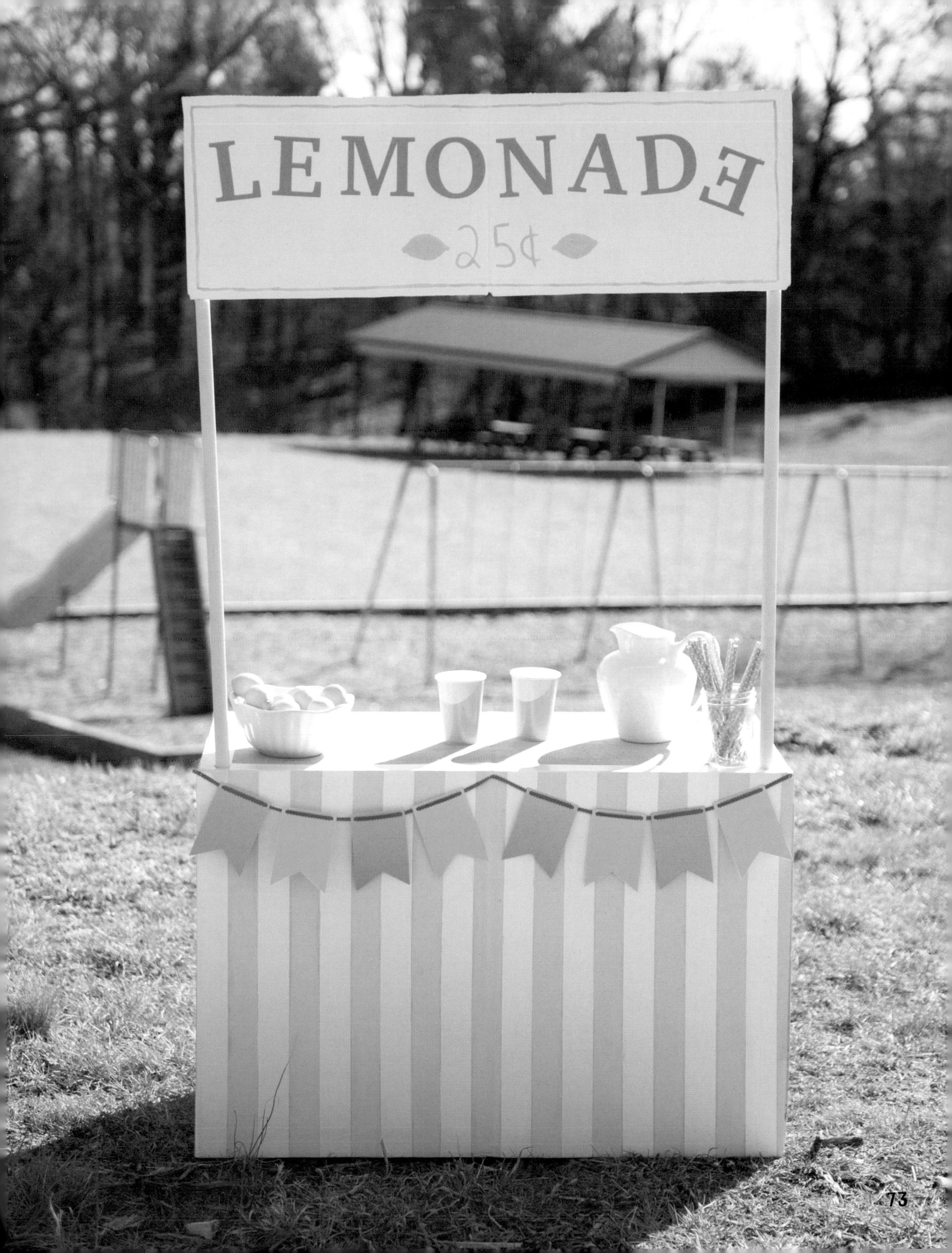
LEMONADE
25¢

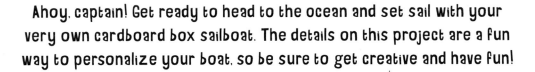

sailboat

Ahoy, captain! Get ready to head to the ocean and set sail with your very own cardboard box sailboat. The details on this project are a fun way to personalize your boat, so be sure to get creative and have fun!

Using your imagination, there are plenty of adventures to be had and new destinations to discover. "Oh, the places you'll go..."

Supply List

- 2 cardboard boxes (24" x 18" x 18")
- Roll of painters' tape
- Wood glue
- Crafting knife
- Pencil or fine-tip, black permanent marker
- Yardstick
- Empty wrapping paper tube (about 1½" x 40")
- Washi tape (assorted colors and patterns)
- 5 to 10 sheets of blue colored card stock (optional)
- Sheet of card stock (optional—your choice of color)
- Paint(s)

The paints you choose for this project will be used for the body of the boat and the mast holder. You can choose a neutral color so the colorful details really pop, or you can choose something a bit flashier.

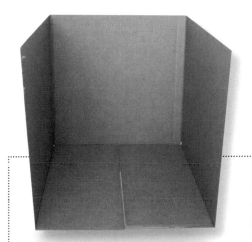

Step 1 Remove the flaps from the top of both boxes with a crafting knife. Then cut out an 18" wide side (including the bottom flap) from each box, and place one box aside.

Step 2 To form the back end of the boat, tape the bottom flaps of the remaining box down with painters' tape. Next use the painters' tape to attach the box set aside in step 1 to the back end of the boat, with the open sides of each box facing each other. This will now serve as the front of the boat.

Step 3 Now cut out the remaining side of the front of the boat as well as the bottom flaps with the crafting knife.

Step 4 To make the boat a bit shallower, remove some cardboard from the top. First draw a line across the entire boat that measures about 5" from the top with a pencil or permanent marker. Then take a crafting knife, and cut on the line to remove the top portion.

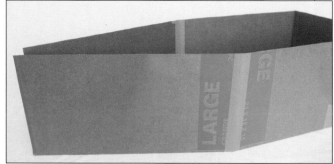

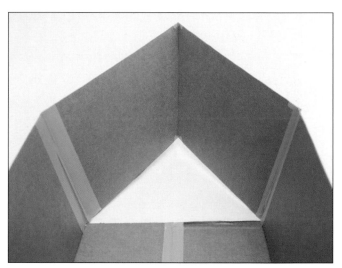

Step 5 To make the bow (also known as the curved front end), flip the boat onto its side, and draw a diagonal line on the front box, starting from the top corner. Then cut along the line with a crafting knife. Repeat this step for the opposite side.

Step 6 Join the diagonal edges together using painters' tape (this will leave a triangular opening at the front end of the boat's floor).

Step 7 Flip the boat over, grab a spare cardboard piece that's at least 18" x 18", and place it over the triangular opening. Trace the triangle with a pencil or permanent marker, and cut out the shape with a crafting knife. Finally, place the triangle over the opening, securing with painters' tape.

Step 8 To make the mast holder, grab three box flaps, and glue them to each other with wood glue. *Let the glue dry at least 30 minutes before handling.*

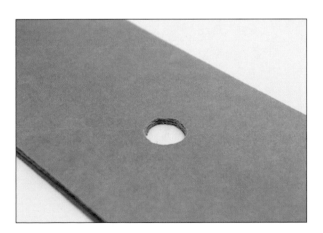

Step 9 Grab the wrapping paper tube, place it upright at the center of the mast holder, and trace it, creating a circle that's the same size as the tube. Use a crafting knife to cut the circle out.

Step 10 Apply wood glue the shorter edges of the mast holder, and place it at the center of the boat, about 4½" from the top. (This will force the boat to "stretch" wider.) *Let the glue dry for at least 1 hour.*

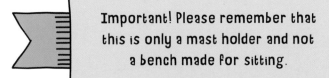

Important! Please remember that this is only a mast holder and not a bench made for sitting.

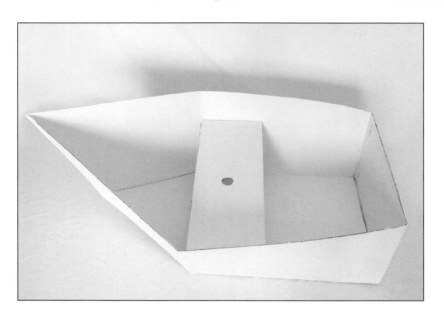

Step 11 Now you can start applying paint! Paint at least three coats of your chosen color on the exterior and interior of the boat. *Be sure to let each coat dry for at least 15 minutes before continuing.*

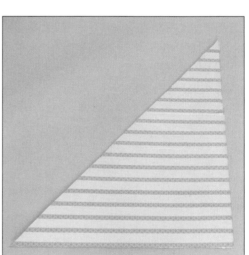

Step 12 With the mast holder in place and paint now dry, it's time to create and attach the boat's sail! To make the sail, take spare cardboard, and cut out a triangle with sides that measure about 22" x 17½" x 28". Now apply three coats of paint to the sail and mast. *Let each coat dry for at least 15 minutes.*

Step 13 Apply wood glue to the back edge of the sail, and attach it to the top of the mast. *Let the glue dry for at least 2 hours before handling.*

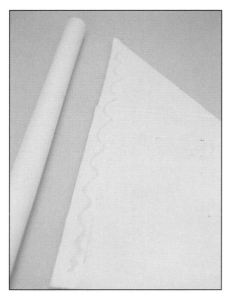

Step 14 Once dry, slide the mast and sail through the mast holder, about 3" down. Rub some wood glue around the mast where it meets the mast holder (both above and below). Then apply painters' tape to the mast to keep it from moving. *Let the glue dry overnight.*

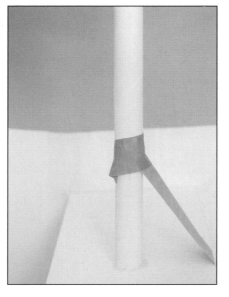

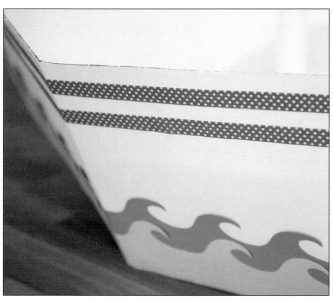

Step 15 Now the fun part—adding the colorful details! Add a few different styles of washi tape to the interior and exterior of the boat and a fun wave pattern to the bottom. Finally, add a small flag made from card stock to the back of the sail. Now imagine the wind in your hair, the open ocean, and the seawater splashing against the boat. Time to set sail!

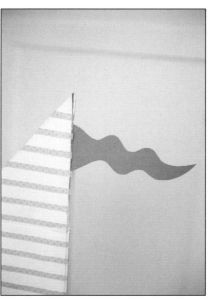

Remember you can use whatever paint colors you want for the body, interior, and sail. You can even paint the mast holder a different color too!

about the author

A stay-at-home mom of three boys, Courtney Sanchez began crafting as a way to keep her children stimulated and active. Being creative with children through imaginative play and the exploration of textures and colors is a great way to bond and teach at the same time.

Courtney's website, craftsbycourtney.com, explores a variety of activities and how-to kids crafts to keep children inspired through creative play.